GET READY TO READ

GET SET, GO!

PRESCHOOL READING READINESS ACTIVITIES

RECOMMENDED FOR AGES 4 AND 5

PREPARED BY BANK STREET COLLEGE MEDIA GROUP

AUTHORS
William H. Hooks
Betty D. Boegehold
Barbara Brenner
Joanne Oppenheim
Seymour V. Reit

Illustrated by Joel Schick

New York / London / Toronto / Sydney

Young children learn best through play. Using all their senses, they eagerly explore the world of things and people. Work and play are not separate or opposite activities to children. Whether they are playing "house," "doctor," "space," or "school," children are stretching their knowledge of the world and themselves, and building "can-do" attitudes about learning. The **Barron's Bunny Activity Books** have been designed with this blending of work/play/learning in mind. With your participation, these activities can provide a way to "play school" and at the same time to practice skills your child will need.

In **Get Ready to Read** you will need to help your child by reading directions and responding to any questions the child may have. Allow enough time for your child to experiment and do some problem solving. Try to expand the concepts in the book to everyday activities. For instance, together you can start noticing signs, finding words that begin with your child's initials, playing rhyming games. It is important to continue using this play-game atmosphere. Keep in mind, too, that nothing builds a child's love of books more than reading storybooks every day. Remember, whether you are reading, playing games, doing activity pages, or explaining "why," an interested child learns more and faster than one who feels pressured to perform. So, easy does it. Take your cues from the child; don't rush, and don't extend any activity period beyond the child's willing attention span.

As parents, we need to communicate to youngsters the high regard that we hold for learning. Young children have extraordinary antennae for picking up on what adults value and cherish. So how we present the **Barron's Bunny Activity Books** to children is very important. These activities are not meant to replace active play, but rather to provide a pleasant sit-down quiet time for sharing. While the books are designed to reinforce specific skills such as following directions, matching, sorting, and categorizing, they should never be presented as required drill. Don't worry if circles are lopsided and lines are wobbly. Children need lots of experience in free drawing to develop small motor skills. Keeping the fun in the activities, being helpful but nonjudgmental, providing lots of praise and support, are more important than demanding perfect results from your preschool child. Keep this early learning a pleasant extension of your child's rich play life.

Enjoy this book with your child. Keep the fun in these activities and the learning will follow suit.

Bank Street College
Media Group

But first, Funny Bunny wants you to write your name.
(Or have someone help you.)

My name: _____

Puff Tail wants you to write your age.

My age: _____

Hop Hop wants you to draw a hat on Funny Bunny.

JUST ALIKE WITH PUFF TAIL

Draw lines between the things below that are just **alike**.

Draw lines between all the things that match.

COLOR THE PICTURE

All the way to the vacation cottage, the bunnies played matching games.

FUNNY BUNNY'S MATCH THE TWINS GAME

Find all the twins in these rows. Then draw a line between each matching pair of bunnies.

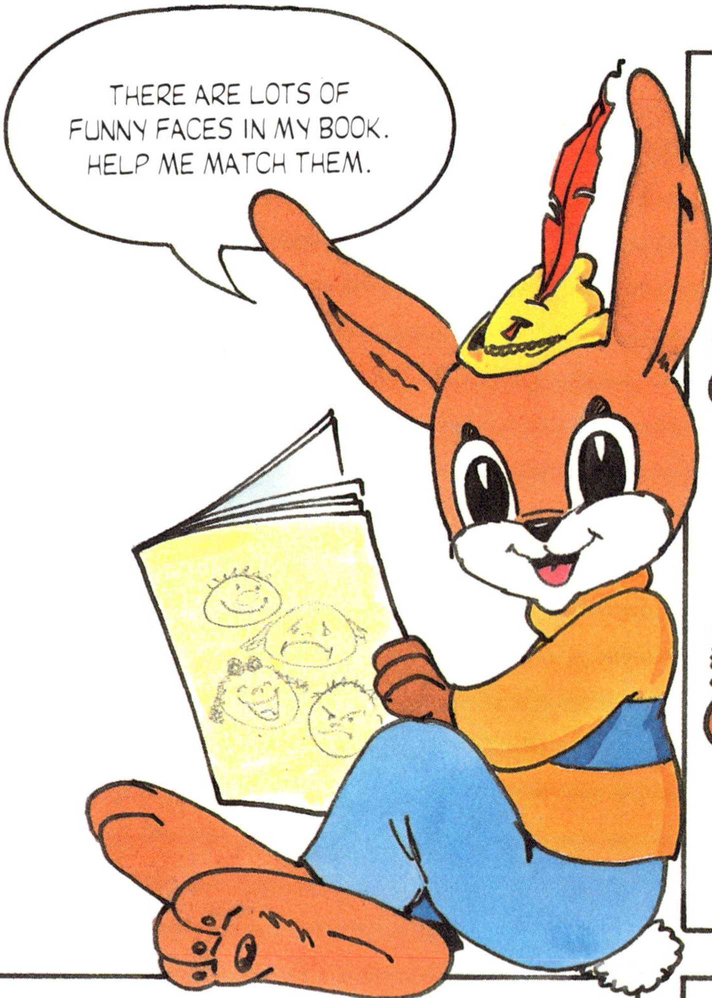

Draw a line to connect the laughing faces.

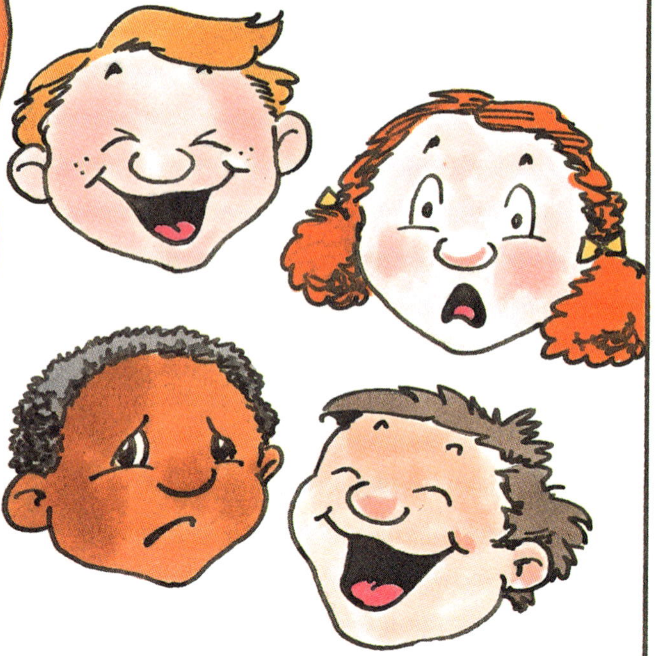

Draw a line to connect the crying faces.

Draw a line to connect the angry faces.

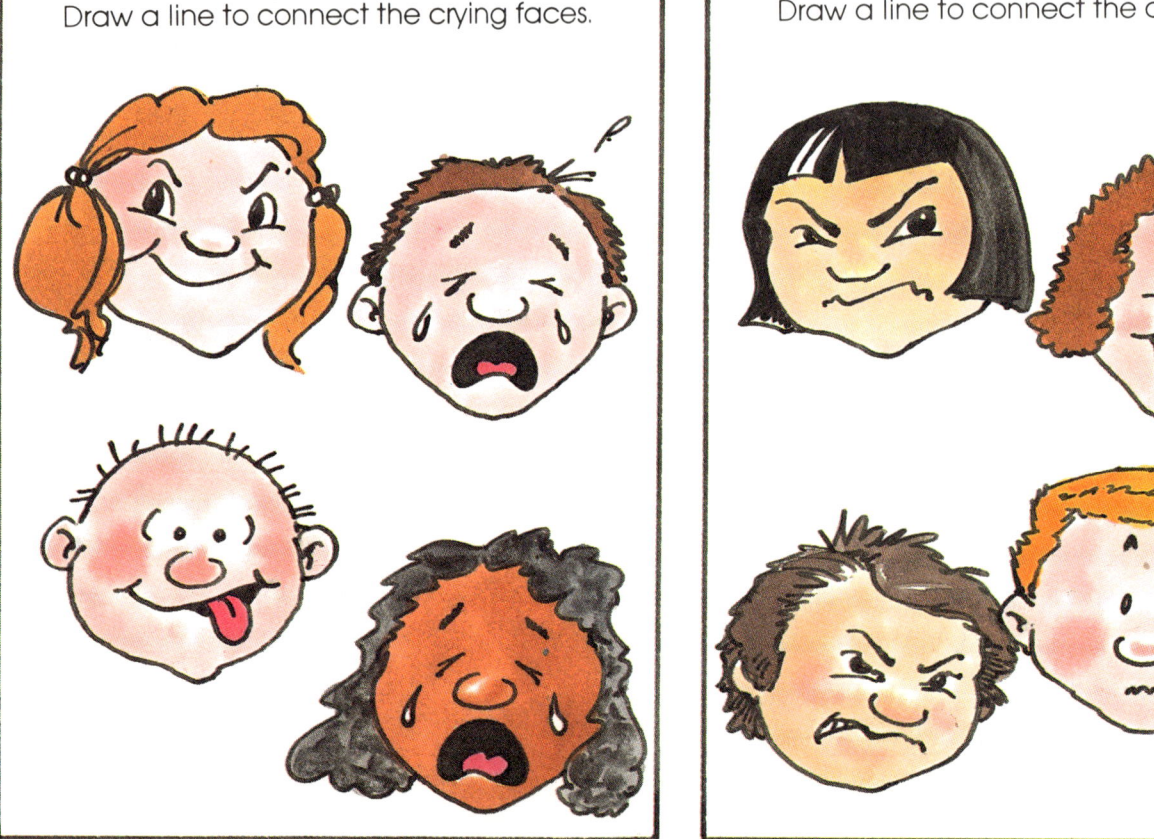

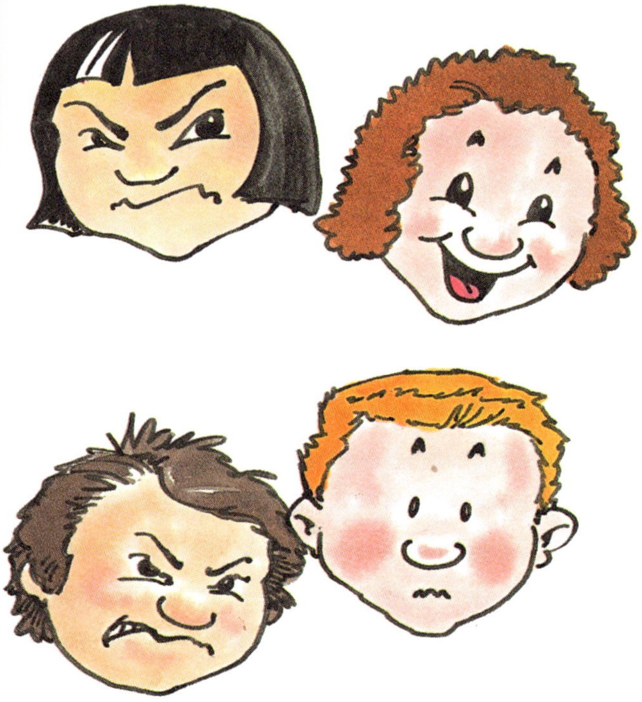

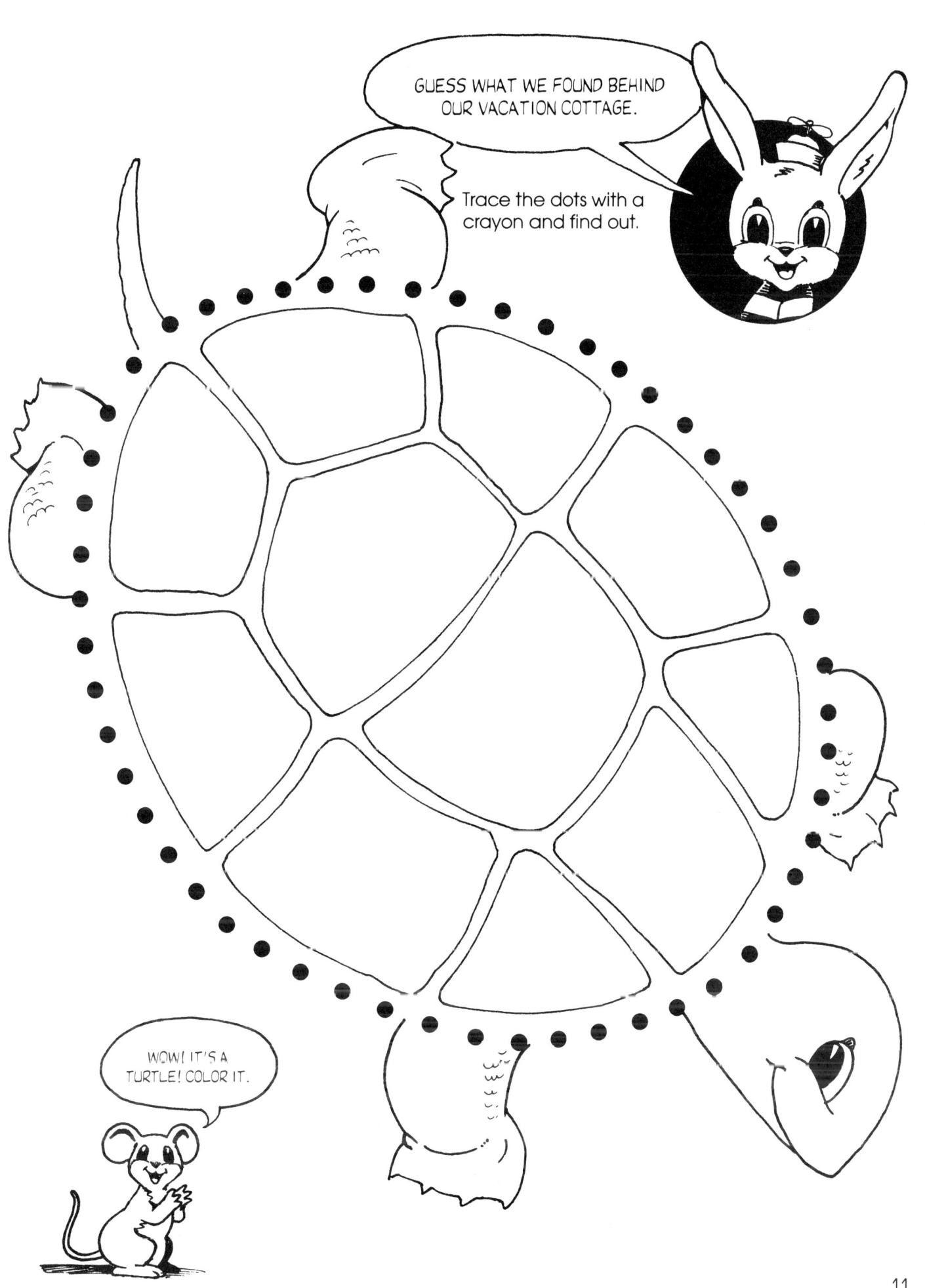

SEEING DIFFERENCES

Puff Tail uses his sharp eyes to find the one thing in each row that is **different** from all the rest. He put an **X under** it.

LET'S PLAY SOME SHARP EYES GAMES. YOU NEED SHARP EYES TO READ.

THE FIRST SHOE HAS 3 STRIPES AND NO LACES.

Now you put an **X under** the one picture that is different in each row.

PUFF TAIL'S SHARP EYE GAME

Find the different bear and put an **X under** it.
Find the different fish and put an **X under** it.
Find the different flower and put an **X under** it.

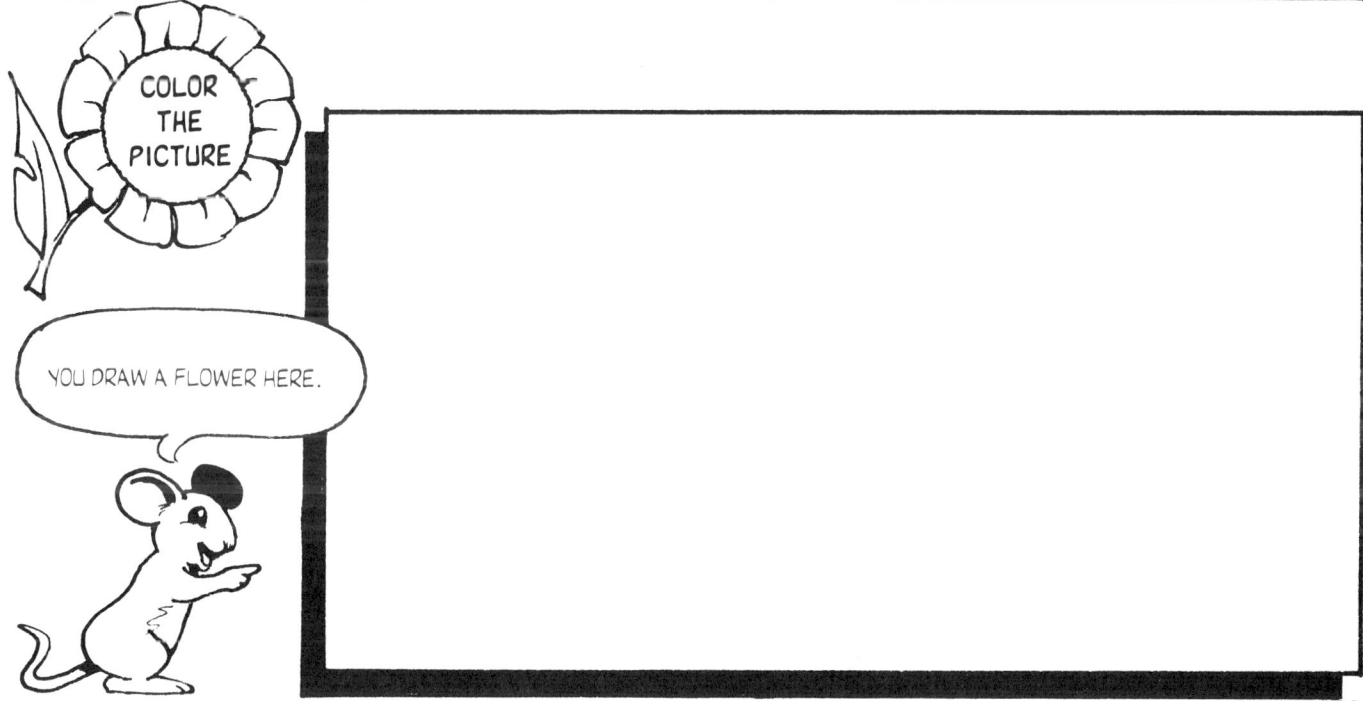

HOP HOP'S SHARP EYE CIRCUS GAME

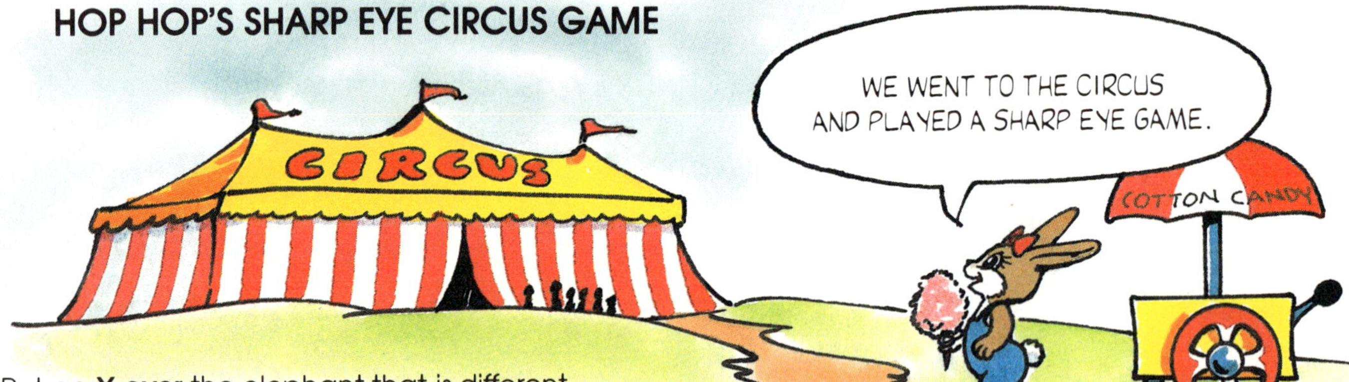
CIRCUS
WE WENT TO THE CIRCUS AND PLAYED A SHARP EYE GAME.
COTTON CANDY

Put an **X over** the elephant that is different.

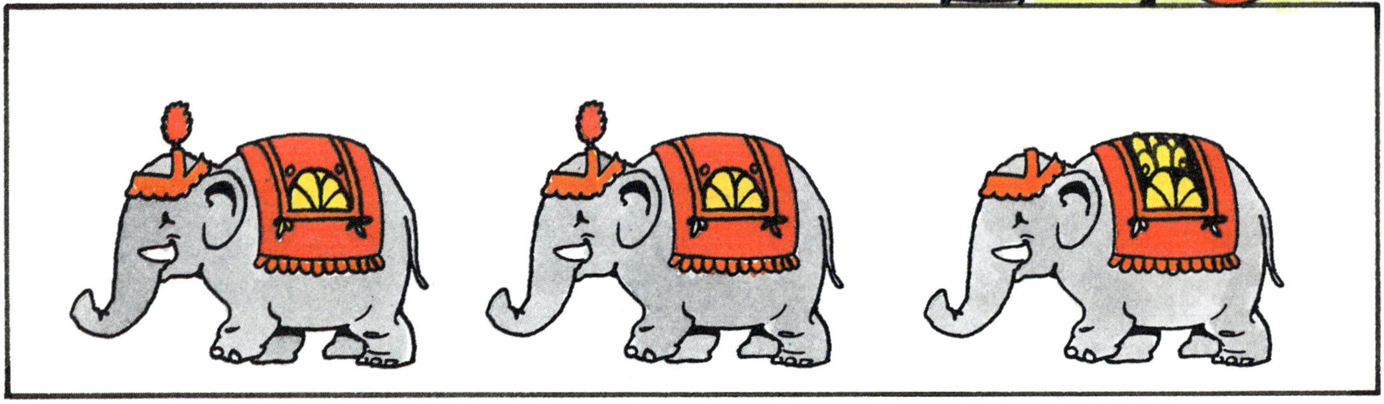

Put an **X over** the seal that is different.

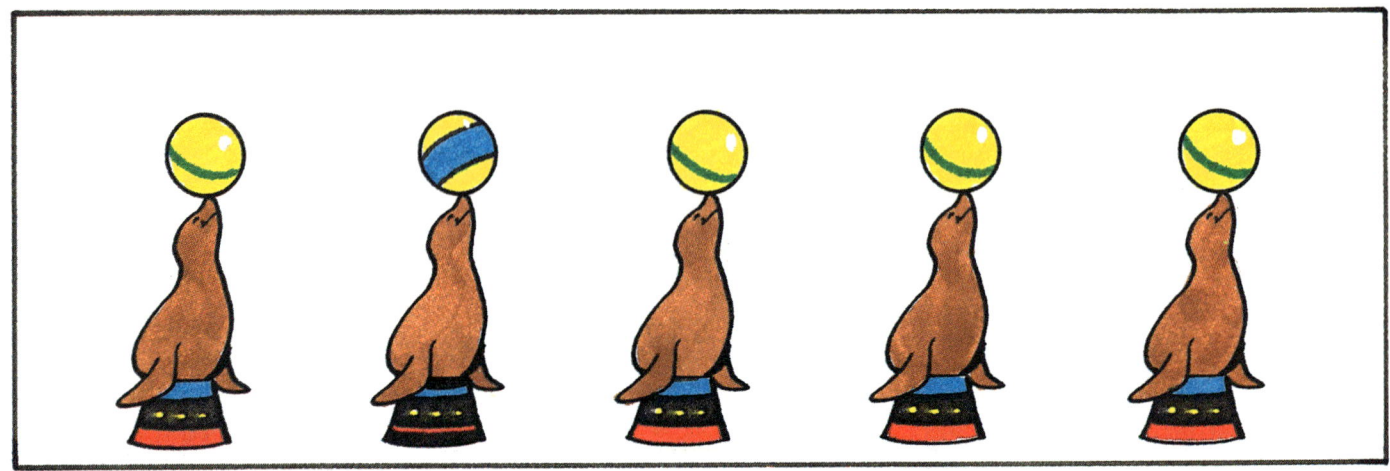

Put an **X over** the monkey that is different.

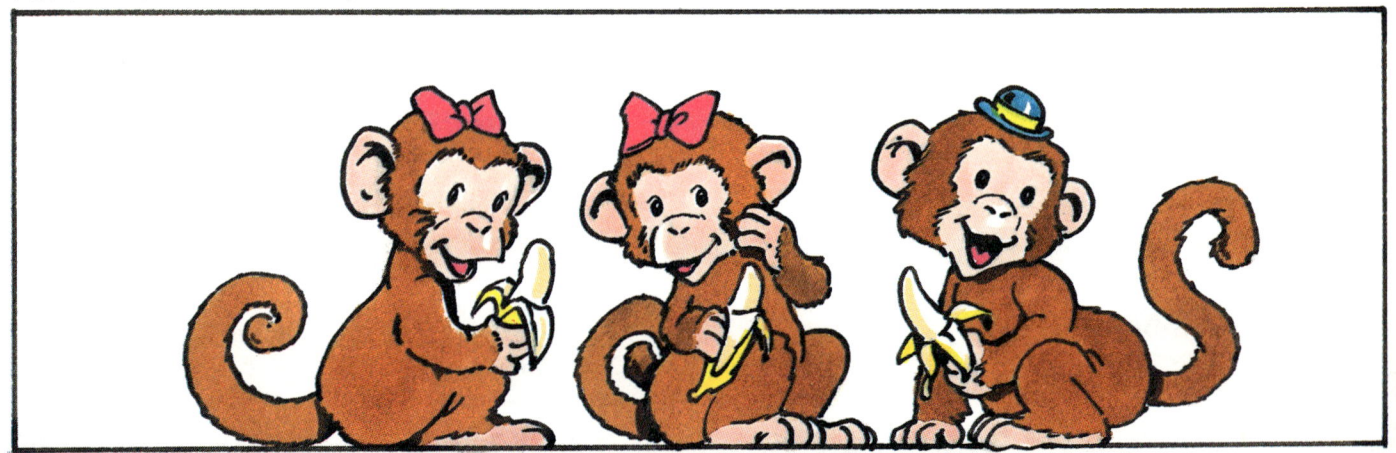

FUNNY BUNNY'S SHARP EYE CIRCUS GAME

I LIKE TO PUT AN **X UNDER** EACH THING THAT IS DIFFERENT, LIKE THIS:

Put an **X under** the clown that is different.

Put an **X under** the tiger that is different.

15

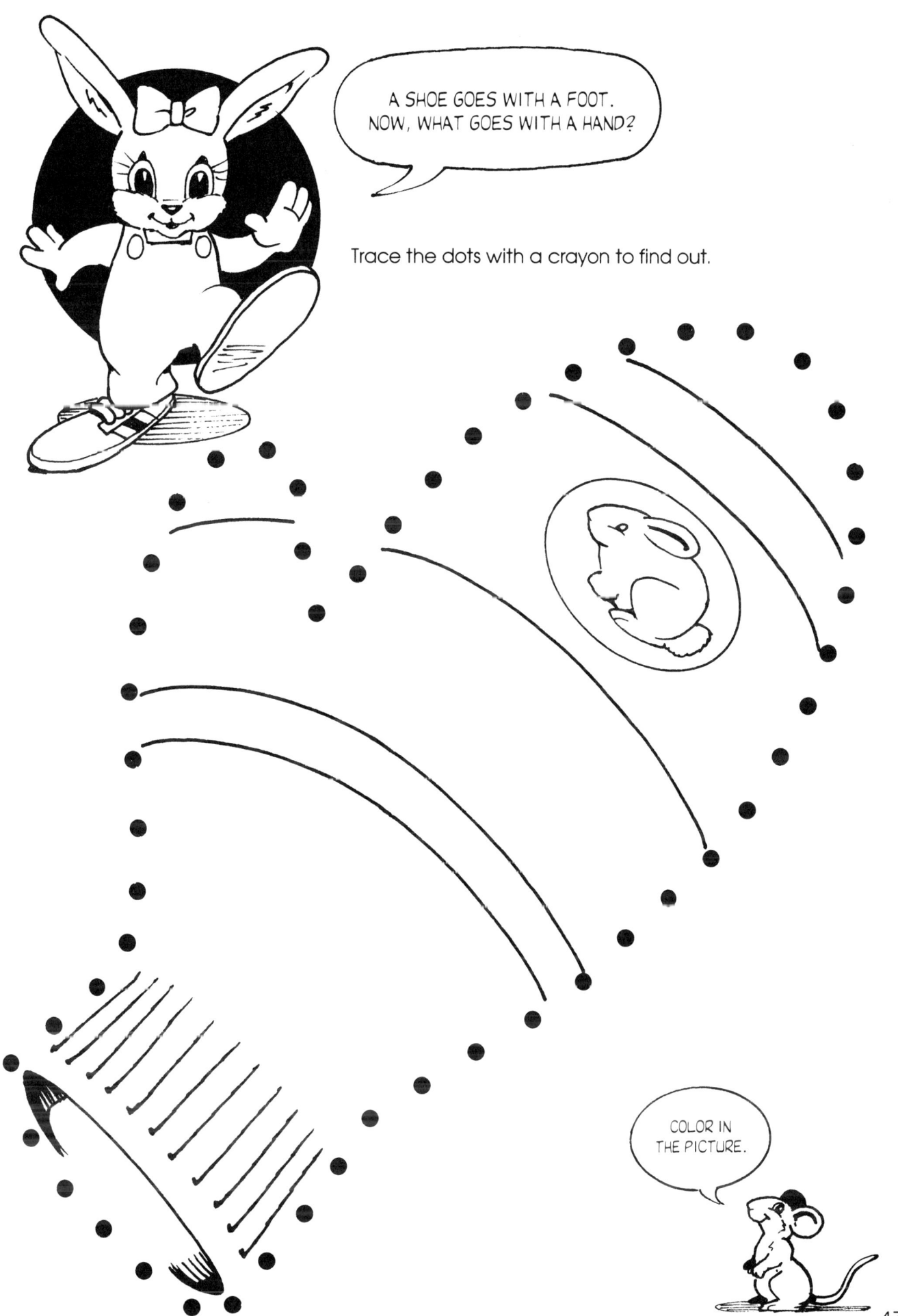

PUFF TAIL'S GO-TOGETHER GAME

Draw a line between the people and things that go together:

HOP HOP'S GO-TOGETHER GAME

Draw a line from each worker to the tool the worker needs.

I NEED A CRAYON WHEN I DRAW A PICTURE. WHAT DO THESE WORKERS NEED?

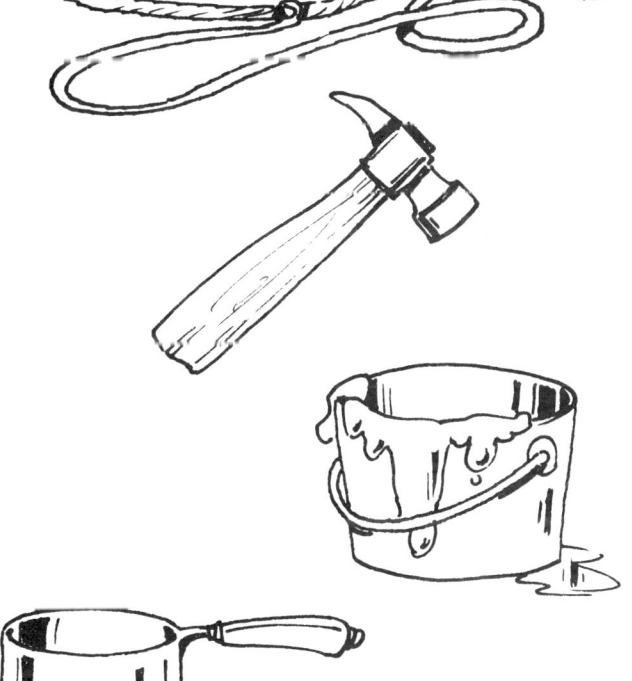

DRAW SOMETHING YOU LIKE TO WORK WITH.

The bunnies are going on a picnic at the zoo.
Help Hop Hop fill the picnic basket.
She wants these four things:

In the picture, draw a line from each thing Hop Hop wants to her basket.

AT THE ZOO

Help Funny Bunny find the biggest and smallest animals in each row.

Put an **X under** the biggest animal in each row.
Put a **circle** ◯ **around** the smallest animal in each row.

Hop Hop hopped to the zoo. She saw 3 big animals and 4 little animals. Put an **X under** the big animals.

NAME THESE ANIMALS.
PUT AN **X UNDER** THE BIGGEST ANIMAL IN EACH BOX.
PUT A CIRCLE ◯ **AROUND** THE SMALLEST ANIMAL IN EACH BOX.

GOOD READERS KNOW THE DIFFERENCE BETWEEN BIG AND LITTLE.

Elephants

Mice

Giraffes

Dogs

Lions

Cats

READING SIGNS

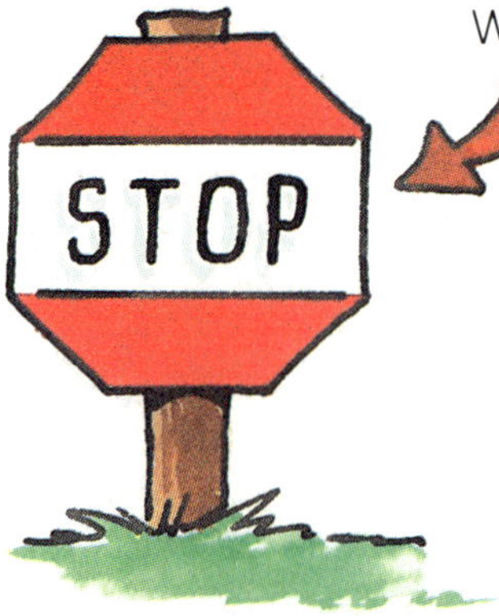

ON THE WAY HOME FROM THE ZOO WE SAW LOTS OF SIGNS.

What does the word on this sign mean?

Trace the word that is on the sign.

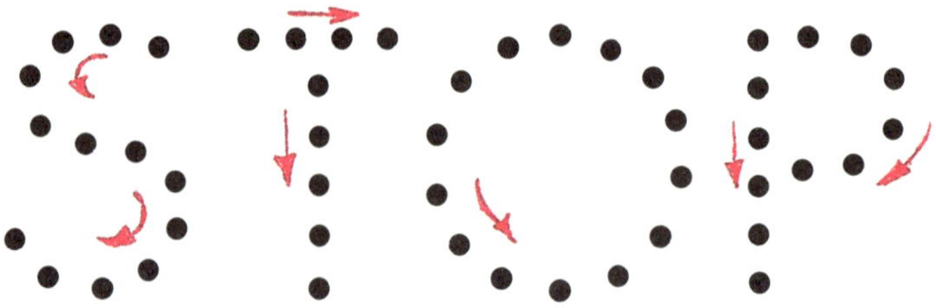

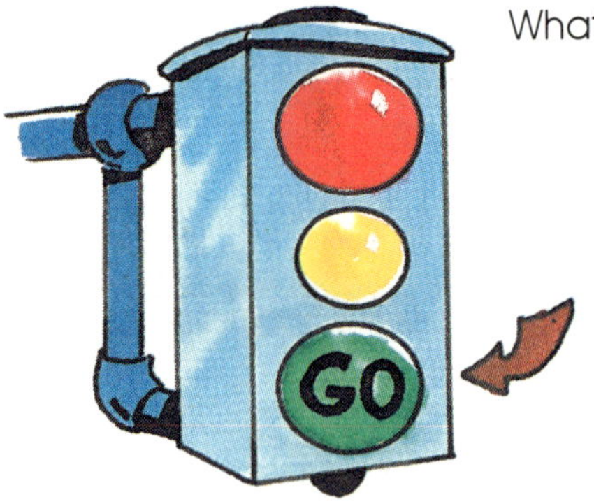

What does the word on this sign mean?

Trace the word that is on the sign.

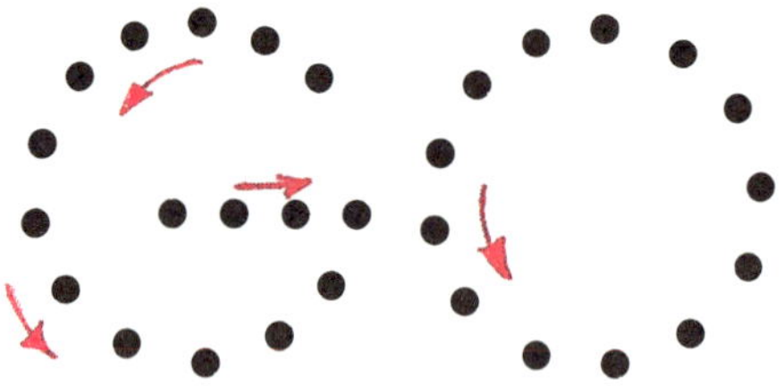

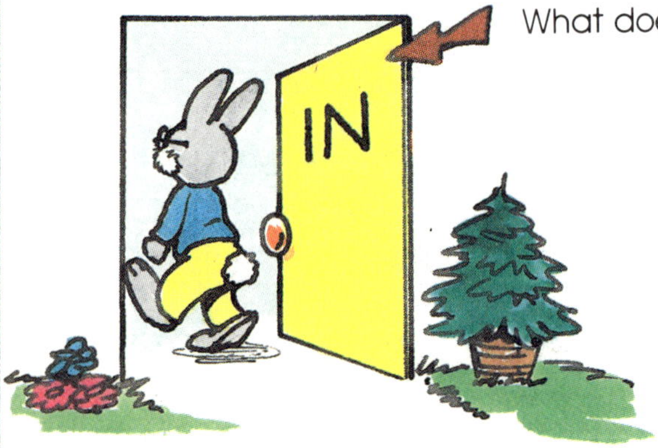

What does the word on this door mean?

Trace the word that is on the door.

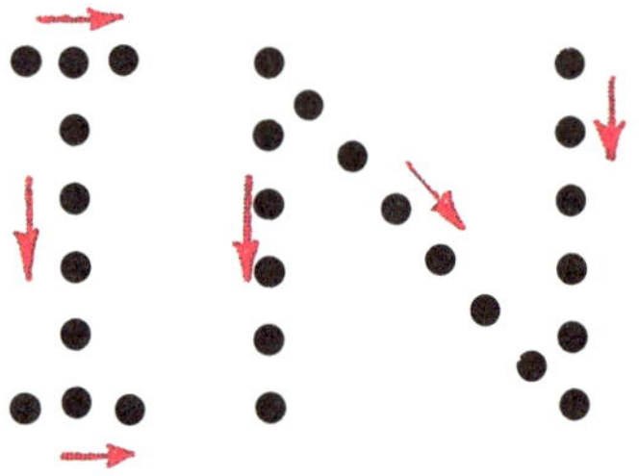

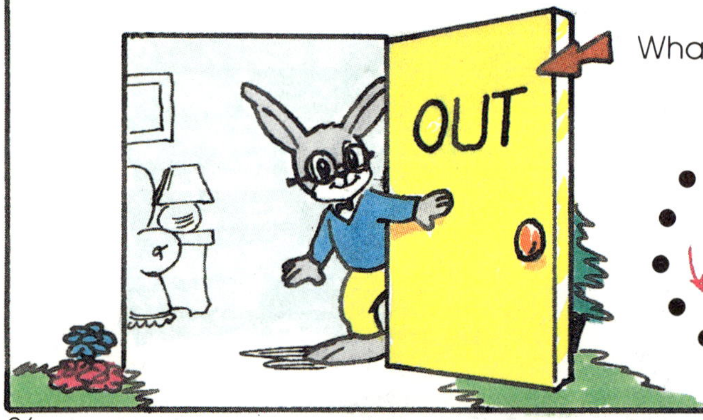

What does the word on this door mean?

Trace the word that is on the door.

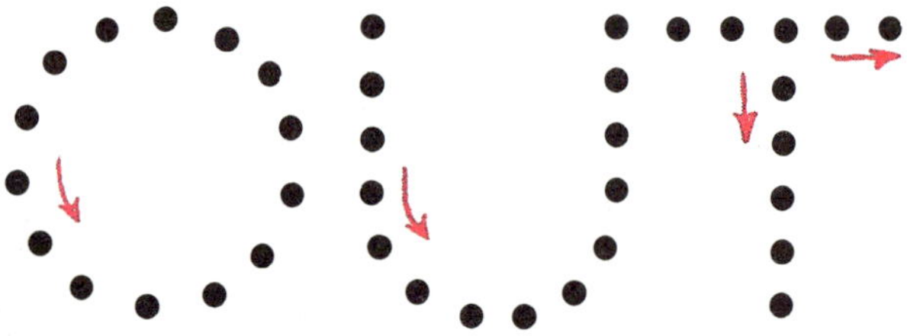

I'M HUNGRY!

Put a circle ◯ around all the signs where Hop Hop can find food.

ITSY's ICE CREAM PARLOR

SARA's SHOE STORE

BETTY's FRUIT STORE

BEE BOOK STORE

JOE's HOT DOGS

Here is a sign that means NO-NO! **POISON! DANGER!**
DON'T EAT! DON'T DRINK! DON'T TOUCH!
Trace the dots to make this sign.

POISON   POISON

COLOR THIS PICTURE.

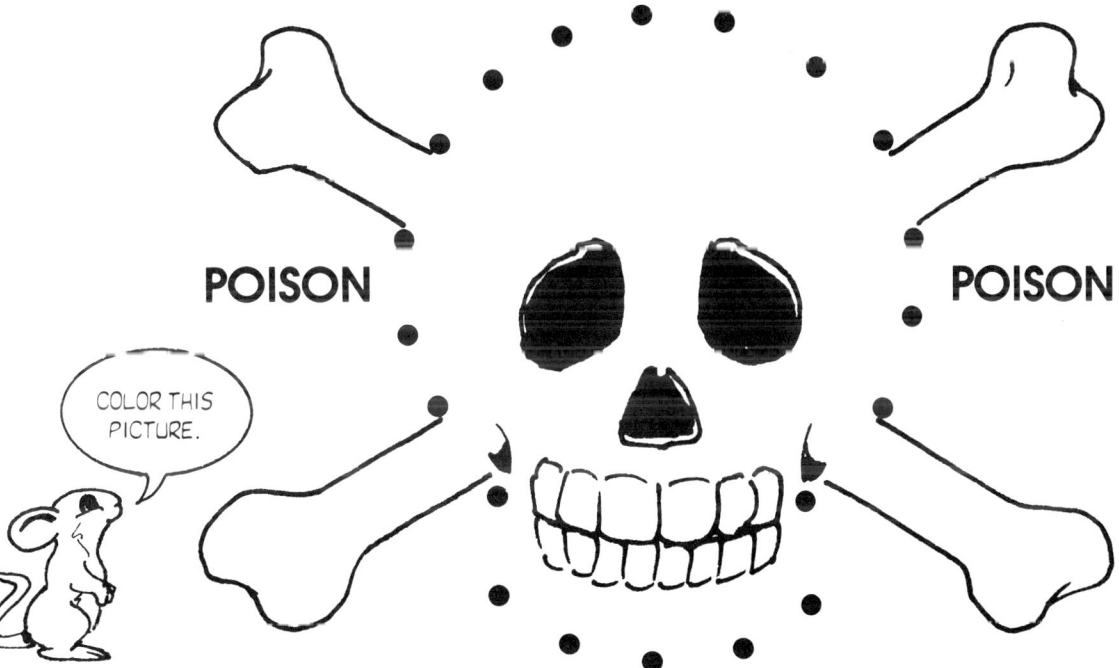

27

I WROTE THREE ZOO POEMS!

Help Funny Bunny read his poems.
Say the word for each picture.

One 1
Two 2
Three 3
A Monkey 
In a Tree

Four 4
Five 5
Six 6
A Bear 
With Sticks

Seven 7
Eight 8
Nine 9
Ten 10
Alligators 
In a Pen

MOTHER GOOSE RHYMES

How much can you read by yourself?
Say the words for the pictures.

Hey diddle diddle,
the 🐱 cat and the 🎻 fiddle

★★

Hickory, dickory, dock,
the 🐭 mouse ran up the 🕰 clock

★★

One 1, two 2 —
buckle my 👞 shoe

★★

Humpty Dumpty
sat on the 🧱 wall

Humpty Dumpty 
had a great fall

DRAW HUMPTY DUMPTY HERE.

MORE PICTURE POEMS

Here are some little poems. You read the pictures. Then draw a circle ◯ around the things in each poem that rhyme.

A BIG 🫏 BILLY GOAT
SAILED AWAY IN A ⛵ BOAT.

AN OLD MAN WITH A 🦯 CANE
RODE OFF IN A 🚂 TRAIN.

I WATERED THE PINK 🌹 ROSE
WITH THE LONG GREEN 🧵 HOSE.

HE WINKED HIS 👁 EYE
AND ATE THE WHOLE 🥧 PIE.

RHYME and COLOR

Help Hop Hop read all the rhymes in this poem. Then help her color in the funny fellow.

THE FUNNY FELLOW

Color the shirt of the funny **fellow YELLOW**.

Color the hair on his **head RED**.

Color his **hands TAN**.

Color one funny **shoe BLUE**.

Color the funny fellow's **sack BLACK**.

Color his **crown BROWN**.

Color his **jeans GREEN**.

NOW COLOR THE REST OF THE FUNNY FELLOW ANY WAY YOU WANT.

THE SURPRISE — A PICTURE STORY

Puff Tail, Hop Hop and Sibble sneaked out of the cottage without Funny Bunny. Why? Tell what is happening in each picture to find out.

My Book

MY BOOK

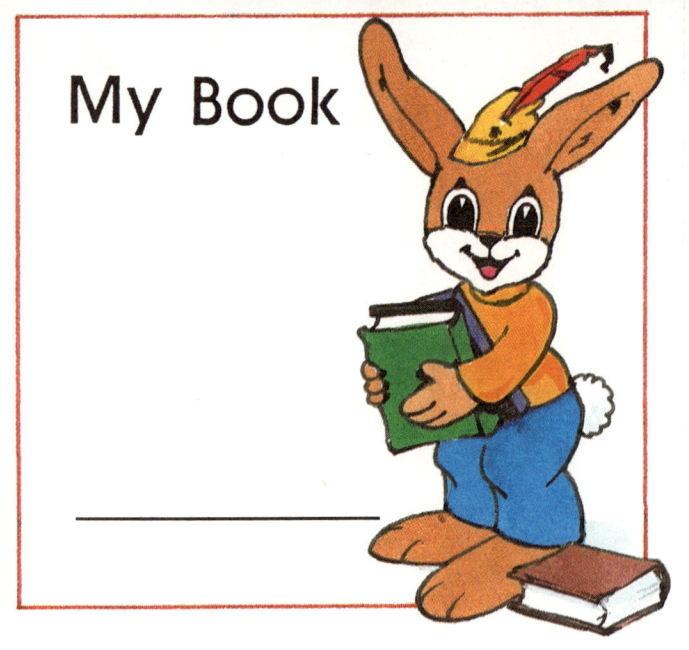

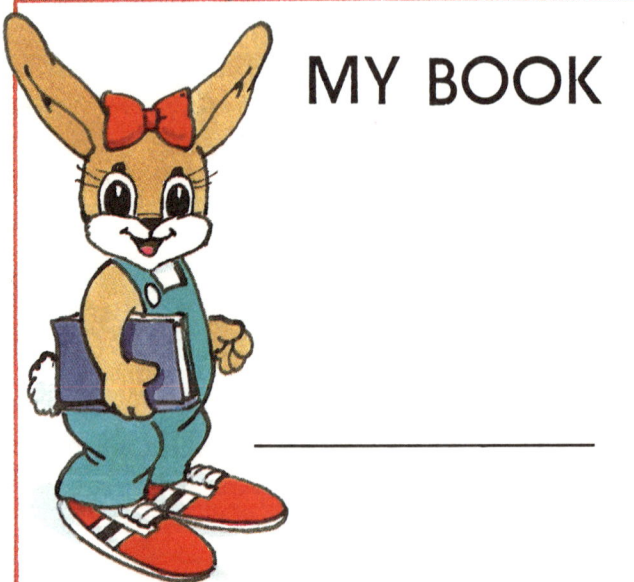

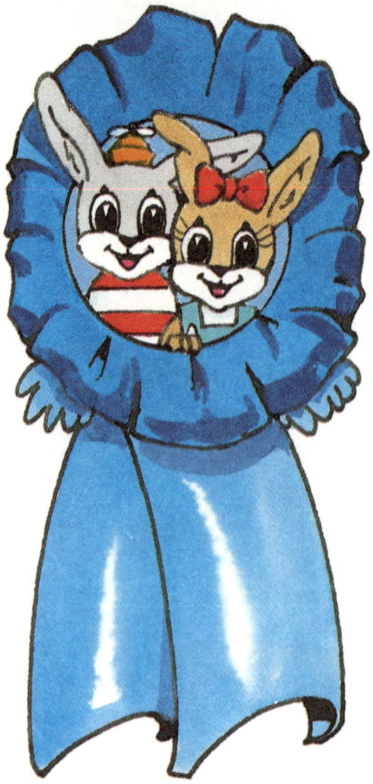

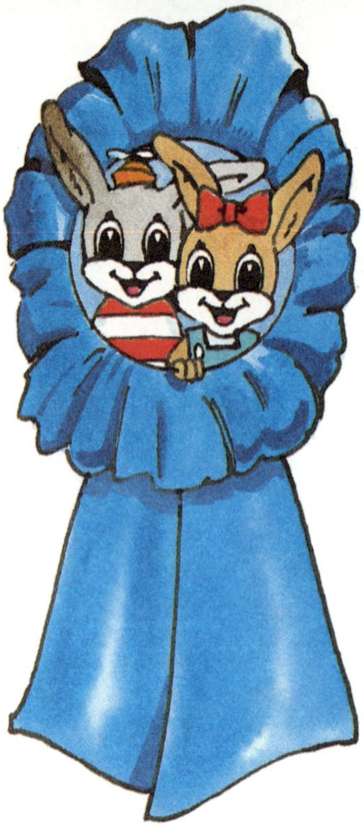

My Book

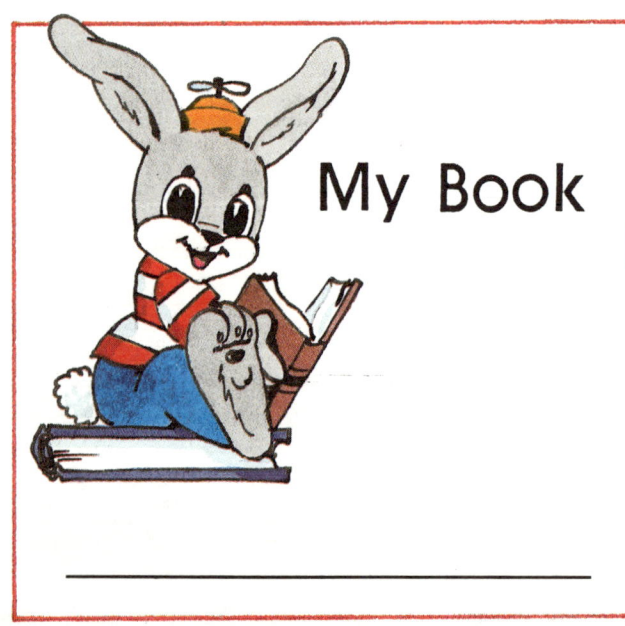

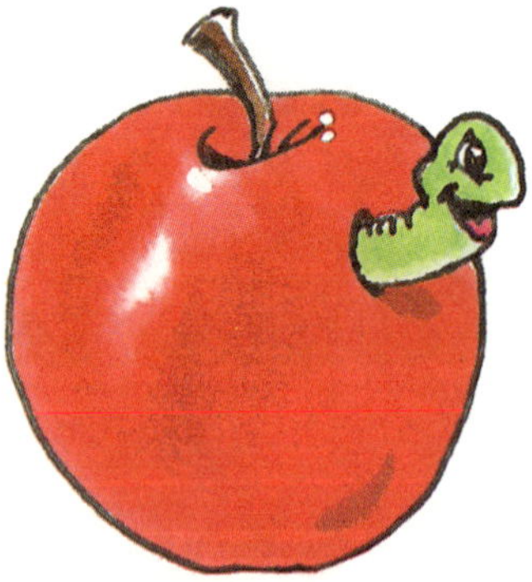

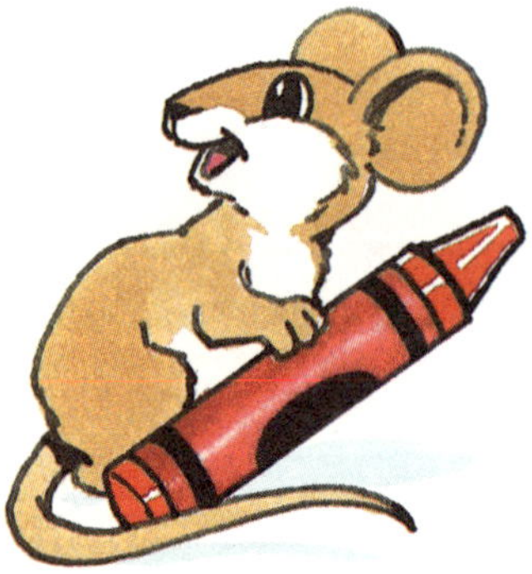

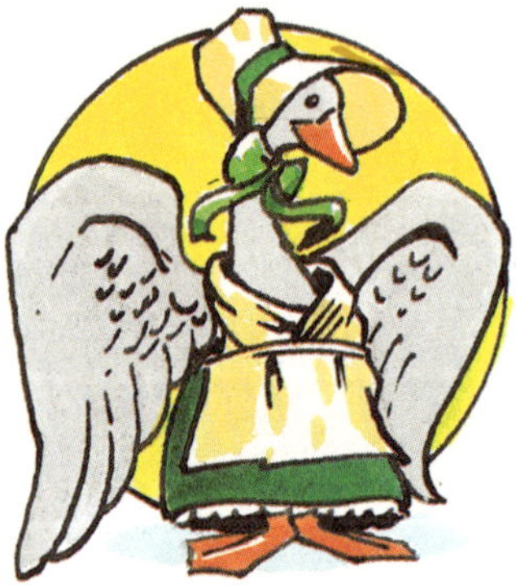

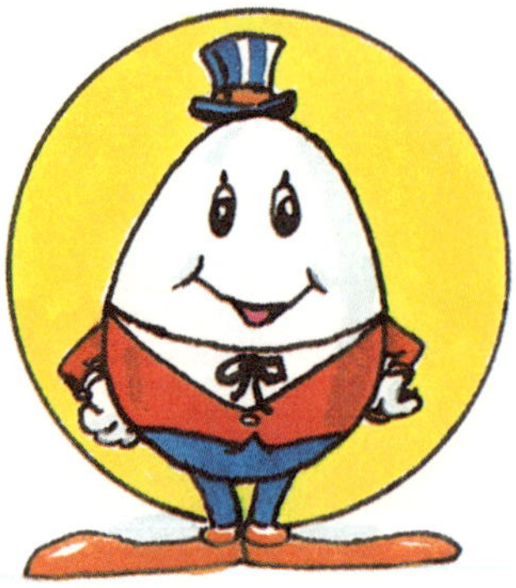

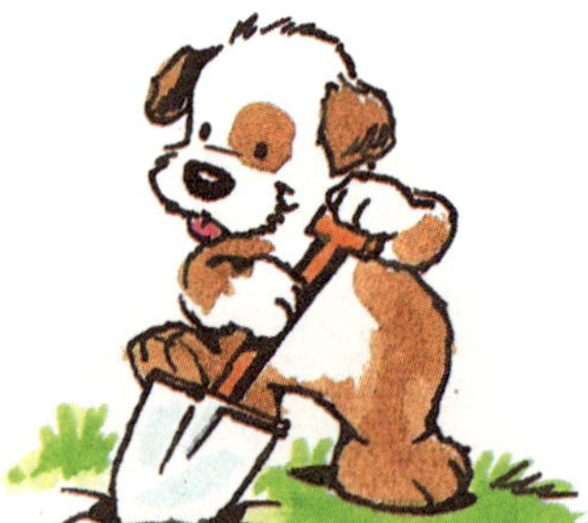

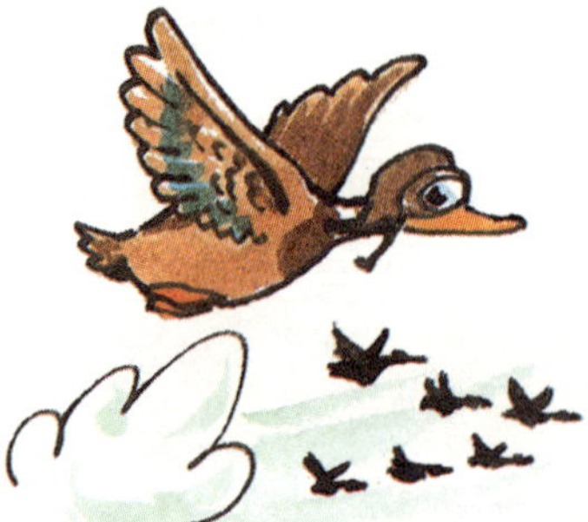

PULL APART STICKERS AND MOISTEN BACK BEFORE USING

Now the bunnies are home again. Tell what is happening in each picture.

Funny Bunny is 5 years old. Connect the dots to make a 5. Color the picture.

33

THE LAST NIGHT OF OUR VACATION WE PLAYED ALPHABET GAMES.

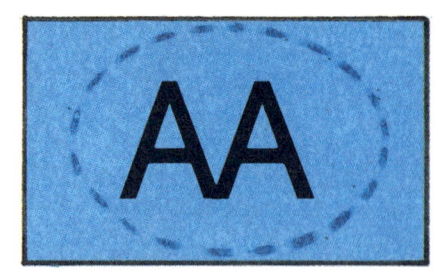

I FOUND THE FIRST PAIR. YOU TRACE THEM.

FUNNY BUNNY'S ALPHABET GAMES

Draw lines around the pairs of cards that are exactly the **same** in each row.

AA	AA	AB
BB	BA	BB
CC	CC	CB
DC	DD	DD
EE	ED	EE

"IN THIS GAME LOOK FOR THE CARD THAT IS DIFFERENT."

"I DID THE FIRST ONE. YOU TRACE IT."

Draw a line around the one card that is **different** in each row.

FF	FF	(EF)
GF	GG	GG
HH	HG	HH
II	II	IH
JH	JJ	JJ

35

FIND THE BLOCKS THAT ARE THE **SAME**.

Draw lines between the blocks that match.

FIND THE PAIRS OF LETTERS THAT ARE **DIFFERENT**.

I DID ONE FOR YOU. TRACE IT.

Look at the banners the bunnies are holding. Cross ✗ out the pair of letters that is different.

PP   PR   PP

QQ   QQ   RQ

RS   RR   RR

SS   SS   SR

TT   TS   TT

COLOR THE BANNERS

37

Draw lines to connect the **matching pairs** of letters.

I DID ONE. YOU TRACE IT.

WE HAVE PLAYED THE WHOLE ALPHABET!

SAY THE WHOLE ALPHABET. MOVE YOUR FINGER UNDER EACH LETTER AS YOU SAY IT.

a b c d e f g h i j
k l m n o p q r s
t u v w x y z

Some letters are missing from the alphabet below. Find the missing letters and trace them in.

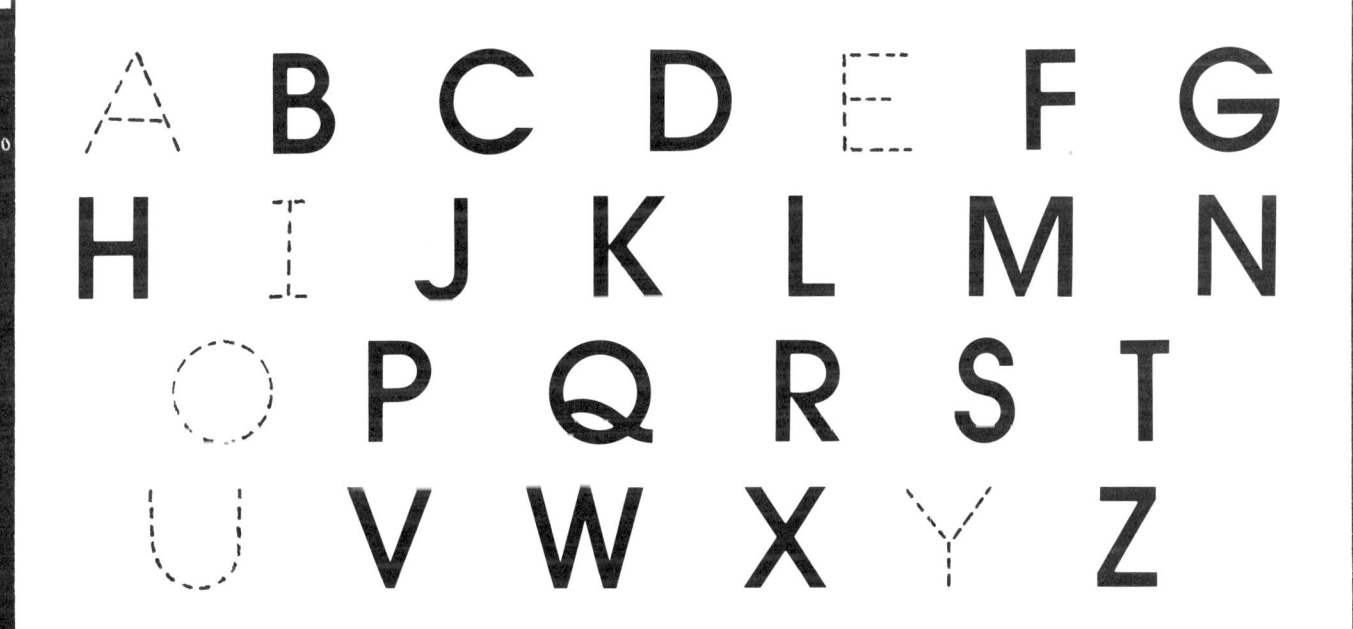

A B C D E F G
H I J K L M N
O P Q R S T
U V W X Y Z

Choose two alphabet letters. Write them below.

_____   _____

39

ALL ABOARD! — A PICTURE STORY

What are the animals doing? Tell what happens in each picture.

Tell what happens in each picture.

Trace the broken lines to find out where the bunnies are. Ask someone to help you read the word.

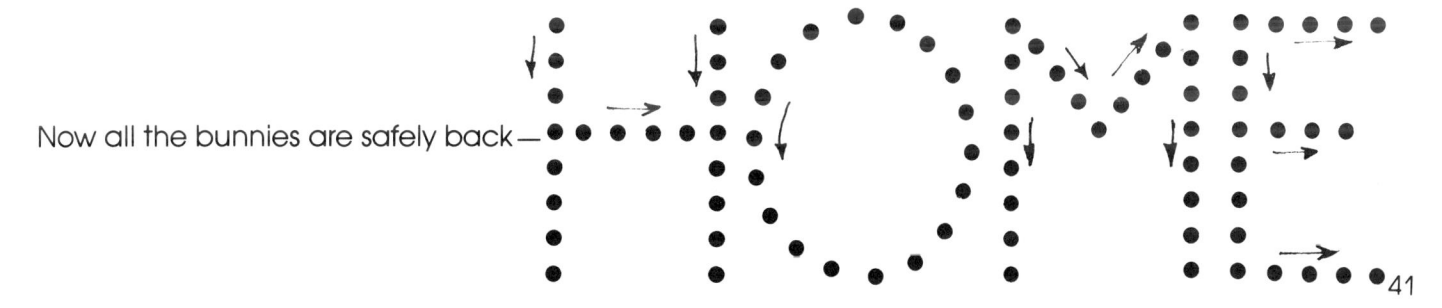

Now all the bunnies are safely back — HOME

41

Hop Hop took some money from her piggy bank. She wants to go to the bookstore. Help her find the way. Draw a line down the path to the bookstore.

START HERE

WHAT DID HOP HOP BUY AT THE STORE?

FOLLOW THE LETTERS IN THE RIGHT ORDER OF THE ALPHABET. START WITH **A** AND GO TO **F**.

Follow the dots. Draw a line from one letter to the next letter.

BUNNY TALES

COLOR THIS PAGE!

Trace this word that tells what Hop Hop is holding.

NAME GAMES

NAMES BEGIN WITH BIG LETTERS. MY NAMES BEGIN WITH A **BIG P** AND A **BIG T**: PUFF TAIL.

GOOD READERS KNOW THE DIFFERENCE BETWEEN **BIG** AND **LITTLE** LETTERS.

Draw a **line under** the big **P**'s.

Draw an **X under** the little **p**'s.

Puff Tail

pumpkin

piano

pig

Trace the big **P**'s and the little **p**'s.

PUFF TAIL'S POTSY GAME

In Puff Tail's Potsy game, look for all the words that start with a little **p**. Draw a little stone like this 🪨 on each space that begins with a little **p**.

START HERE!

pink
boy
party
hop
sing
pony
Puff Tail
pop
put
play
run
pan
girl

I DREW A STONE ON ONE WORD THAT BEGINS WITH A LITTLE P.

Puff Tail is looking for words that begin with the letter **P**.
Draw a circle ◯ around all the words that begin with a big **P** or a little **p**.

BIG P AND LITTLE P HAVE THE SAME SOUND.

PARKING

Puff Tail

pig

woman

bench

boy

path

puppy

ball

shovel

pail

pond

pollywogs

PLEASANT PARK

46

MY PET TURTLE'S NAME IS TOM. IT STARTS WITH THE BIG LETTER T.

Draw a **line under** the big **T**'s.
Draw an **X under** the little **t**'s.

| tent | Tom |
| table | tiger |

COLOR THE PAGE.

Trace the big **T**'s and the little **t**'s.

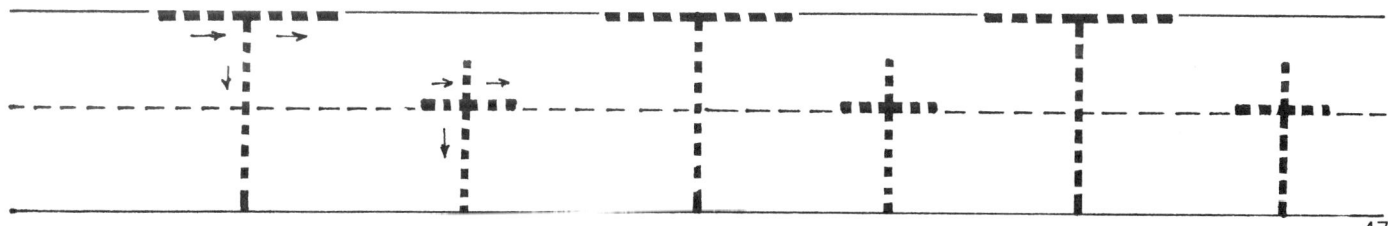

47

MY NAME BEGINS WITH 2 BIG LETTERS: **BIG F** AND **BIG B**.

BIG LETTERS ARE CALLED CAPITAL LETTERS.

Funny Bunny

Trace the big **F**'s and the big **B**'s.

F F F B B B

Draw a circle ◯ around the words beginning with a big **B**.

Billy   ball

box   Beth

Draw a circle ◯ around the words beginning with a big **F**.

fox   Fido

Fred   fan

Trace the big and little **F**'s and **B**'s.

F f F f B b B b

DRAW A CIRCLE ◯ AROUND EACH LETTER THAT IS THE SAME AS THE LETTER IN THE MIDDLE.

F f	B b
F **F** f	B **B** B
f F	B b

BIG AND LITTLE LETTERS MAKE THE SAME SOUND.

Color in the fish.

Make 2 little **f**'s and **b**'s.   Make a big **F**.   Make a big **B**.

Sometimes Hop Hop writes in big letters: HOP HOP
Sometimes Hop Hop writes in small letters: hop hop
But most times Hop Hop uses big and little letters: Hop Hop

BIG LETTERS ARE CALLED CAPITAL LETTERS.

NAMES BEGIN WITH A BIG LETTER.

GOOD READERS KNOW BIG LETTERS FROM LITTLE LETTERS.

Trace Hop Hop's name with your crayon.

FOLLOW THE ARROWS.

HOP HOP

hop hop

Hop Hop

Write your name here.

50

HOP HOP'S H GAME

Hop Hop laid her cards in the shape of an **H**. Draw a circle ◯ around all the card pictures that start with the little letter **h**.

BIG H AND LITTLE H HAVE THE SAME SOUND.

- house
- hamster
- pig
- hat
- cat
- hand
- hot dog
- ball

Draw a picture of a word that begins with a little letter **h**.

YOU CAN USE THE H WORD PICTURES ABOVE.

SCHOOL GAMES

Funny Bunny, Puff Tail and Hop Hop will be going to school soon. They want to play some school games.

FIND THE TWO PICTURES THAT ARE **ALIKE** IN EACH ROW.

THEN COLOR IN THE LITTLE CIRCLES UNDER THE TWO PICTURES THAT ARE ALIKE.

I DID THIS ROW.

You do this one. Color in the circles under the two pictures that are alike.

52

LET'S DO SOMETHING A LITTLE DIFFERENT.

I DID THE FIRST ONE FOR YOU.

MORE SCHOOL GAMES

Color in the circle under the one thing in each row that is **different**.

Now **you** draw something to make one rabbit look different.

COLOR THIS PAGE

53

SCHOOL GAMES

Some words tell what things are.
Name the thing in each picture. Draw a circle ◯ around the letter the word begins with.

I DID ONE FOR YOU. TRACE MINE.

HERE ARE PICTURES OF SOME MORE THINGS.

c d

l t

y q

w v

w m

p y

m n

t f

e a

54

MORE SCHOOL GAMES

Some words tell what things are. Name the thing in each picture. Draw a circle ◯ around the letter the word begins with.

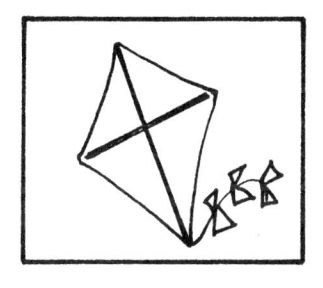

I DID ONE FOR YOU. TRACE MINE.

K   M

F   T

B (S)

T   P

B   F

T   K

M   D

J   H

M   O

Write the first letter in your first name. _____

Write the first letter in your last name. _____

COLOR THE PAGE

55

SCHOOL GAMES

Some words tell what we do. Name what the animal is doing in each picture. Draw a circle ◯ around the letter the word begins with.

climb

dig

"I DID ONE FOR YOU!"

fly

l (c)

x d

f s

swim

eat

jump

r s

f e

p j

paint

smile

run

m p

s d

r t

56

Here's something all rabbits can do. Trace the dots to find out what it is.

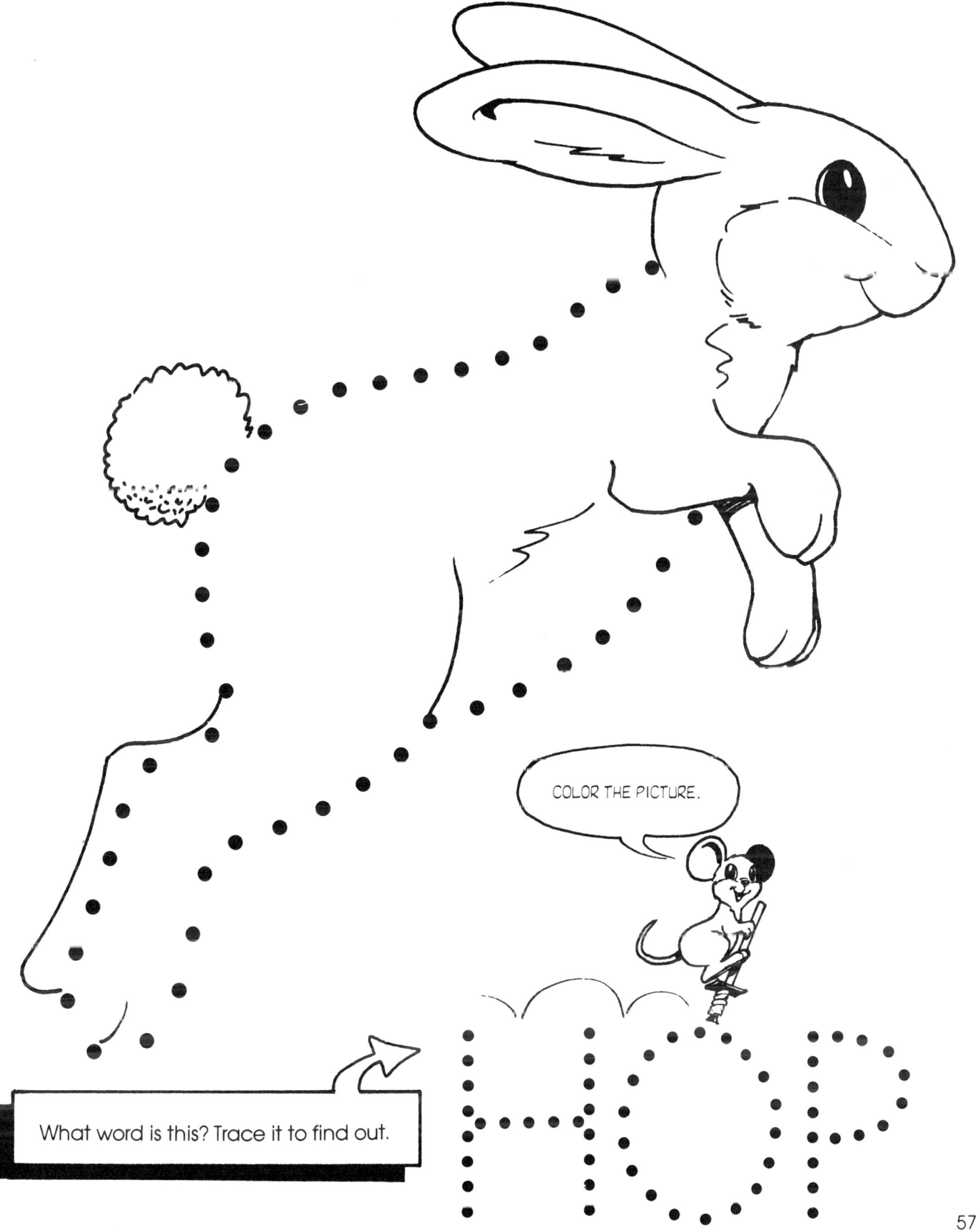

COLOR THE PICTURE.

What word is this? Trace it to find out.

HOP

SCHOOL GAMES

Draw an ✗ **across** the picture that does **not** belong with the rest.

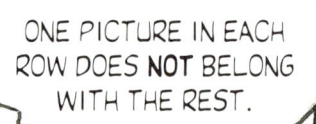

*ONE PICTURE IN EACH ROW DOES **NOT** BELONG WITH THE REST.*

I DID ONE FOR YOU. TRACE THE X.

MORE SCHOOL GAMES

Draw lines across the shapes that are **alike** in each row.

DRAW THE LINES FROM THE TOP CORNER OF THE BOX TO THE BOTTOM CORNER, LIKE THIS:

DRAW SOME SHAPES YOU LIKE HERE.

COLOR THE PICTURES

SCHOOL GAMES

SAY THE NAME OF THE PICTURE OUTSIDE THE FIRST ROW. WHAT SOUND DOES IT START WITH?

I DID THE FIRST ROW FOR YOU.

Put an **X** on the two pictures in each row that start with the **same** sound as the picture outside that row.

snake	tree	sun	ball

fan	flag	ball	hat

flower	cane	cup	fish

hat	pumpkin	dog	doll

60

Four words beginning with the letter **c** are hiding in this tree:

a car   a cat   a carrot   a can

FIND THE 4 PICTURES THAT BEGIN WITH THE LETTER C AND COLOR THEM.

COLOR THE REST OF THE PICTURE

SCHOOL GAMES

Funny Bunny, Hop Hop and Puff Tail have put their names on their lunch boxes. Draw a line from each bunny to his or her lunch box.

Funny Bunny

Hop Hop

Puff Tail

Hop Hop

Funny Bunny

Puff Tail

DRAW ME A LUNCH BOX.

SCHOOL GAMES

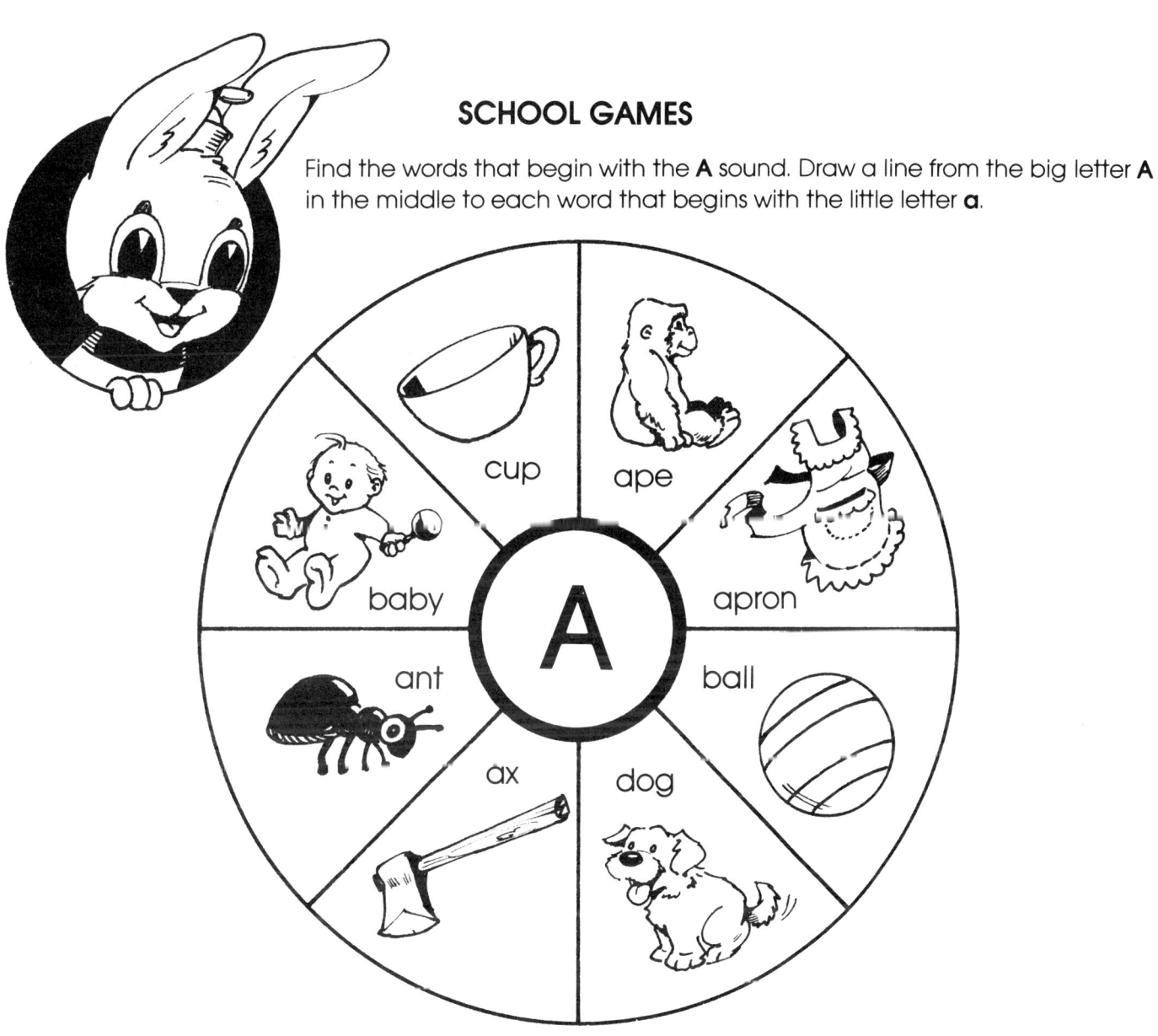

Find the words that begin with the **A** sound. Draw a line from the big letter **A** in the middle to each word that begins with the little letter **a**.

- cup
- ape
- baby
- apron
- ant
- ball
- ax
- dog

A

Trace these dots to make a picture of something that begins with the letter **A**.

COLOR IN THE PICTURE.

63

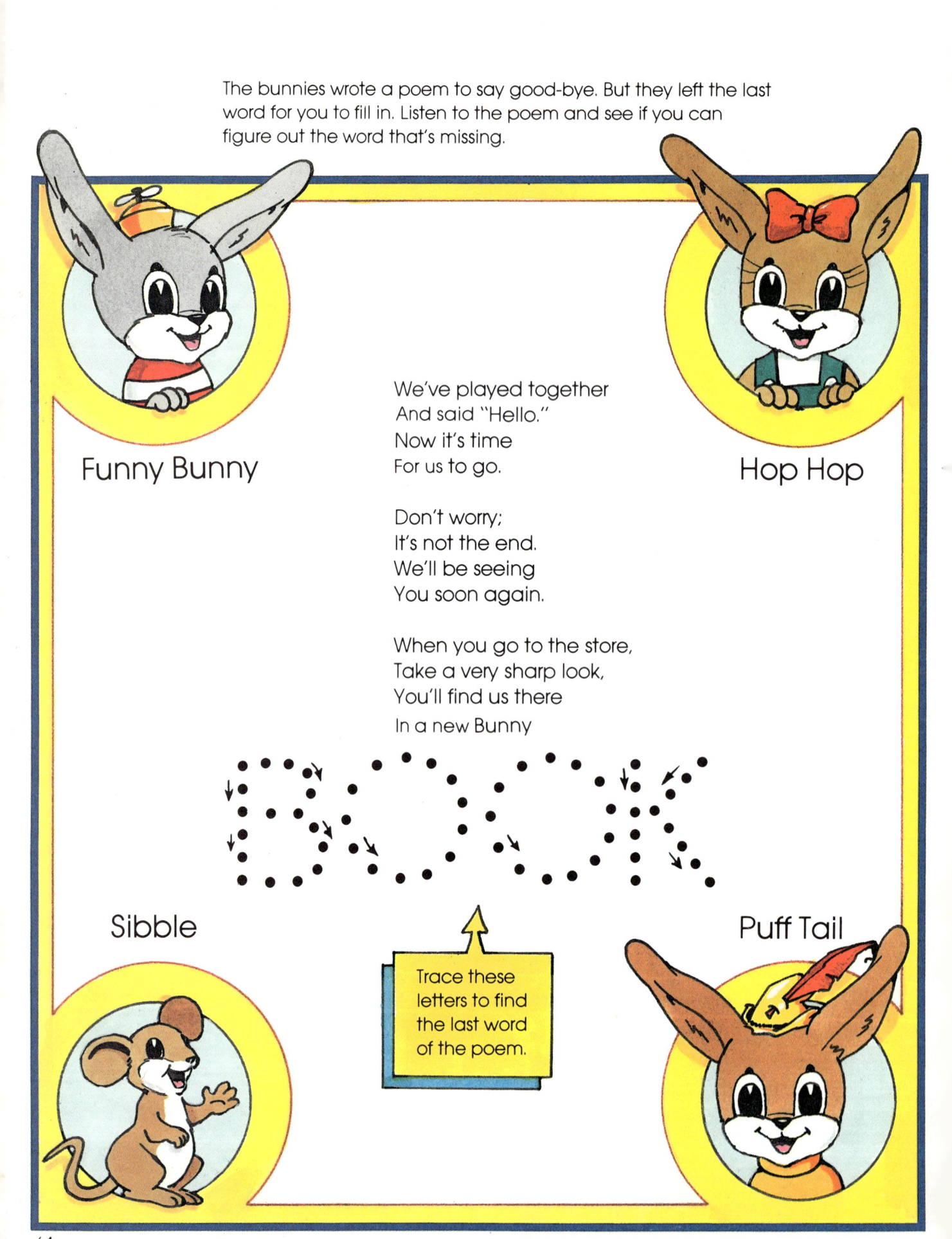

The bunnies wrote a poem to say good-bye. But they left the last word for you to fill in. Listen to the poem and see if you can figure out the word that's missing.

Funny Bunny

Hop Hop

We've played together
And said "Hello."
Now it's time
For us to go.

Don't worry;
It's not the end.
We'll be seeing
You soon again.

When you go to the store,
Take a very sharp look,
You'll find us there
In a new Bunny

BOOK

Sibble

Puff Tail

Trace these letters to find the last word of the poem.

64